WOMEN WHO WIN

Laila Ali

Cynthia Cooper

Lindsay Davenport

Mia Hamm

Martina Hingis

Chamique Holdsclaw

Marion Jones

Anna Kournikova

Michelle Kwan

Lisa Leslie

Gabrielle Reece

Dorothy "Dot" Richardson

Sheryl Swoopes

Venus & Serena Williams

CHELSEA HOUSE PUBLISHERS

WOMEN WHO WIN

Anna Kournikova

Connie Berman

Introduction by
HANNAH STORM

CHELSEA HOUSE PUBLISHERS
Philadelphia

Frontis: The joy of victory. Anna celebrates on the court after a winning shot in the fifth round of the 2001 Australian Open.

CHELSEA HOUSE PUBLISHERS

Editor in Chief: Sally Cheney
Director of Production: Kim Shinners
Production Manager: Pamela Loos
Art Director: Sara Davis
Production Editor: Diann Grasse

Staff for Anna Kournikova
Editor: Sally Cheney
Associate Editor: Benjamin Kim
Associate Art Director: Takeshi Takahashi
Layout by D&G Limited.

The Chelsea House World Wide Web address is
http://www.chelseahouse.com

First Printing

1 3 5 7 9 8 6 4 2

Library of Congress Cataloging-in-Publication Data

Berman, Connie.
  Anna Kournikova / Connie Berman.
   p. cm.—(Women who win)
  Includes bibliographical references (p.) and index.
   Summary: A bibliography of the woman who grew up in Russia in mod-
est circumstances and fulfilled her dream of becoming a top tennis play-
er.
  ISBN 0-7910-6529-7 (alk. paper)—ISBN 0-7910-6530-8 (pbk. alk. paper)
  1. Kournikova, Anna, 1981—Juvenile literature. 2. Tennis players—
Russia (Federation)—Biography—Juvenile literature. 3. Women tennis
players—Russia (Federation)—Biography—Juvenile literature. [1.
Kournikova, Anna, 1981– . 2. Tennis players. 3. Women—Biography.] I.
Title. II. Series.

GV994.K65 B47 2001
796.342'092—dc21
  [B]   2001028965

CONTENTS

WOMEN WHO WIN

Hannah Storm
NBC Studio Host

You go girl! Women's sports are the hottest thing going right now, with the 1900s ending in a big way. When the U.S. team won the 1999 Women's World Cup, it captured the imagination of all sports fans and served as a great inspiration for young girls everywhere to follow their dreams.

That was just the exclamation point on an explosive decade for women's sports—capped off by the Olympic gold medals for the U.S. women in hockey, softball, and basketball. All the excitement created by the U.S. national basketball team helped to launch the Women's National Basketball Association (WNBA), which began play in 1997. The fans embraced the concept, and for the first time, a successful and stable women's professional basketball league was formed.

I was the first ever play-by-play announcer for the WNBA—a big personal challenge. Broadcasting, just like sports, had some areas with limited opportunities for women. There have traditionally not been many play-by-play opportunities for women in sports television, so I had no experience. To tell you the truth, the challenge I faced was a little scary! Sometimes we are all afraid that we might not be up to a certain task. It is not easy to take risks, but unless we push ourselves we will stagnate and not grow.

Here's what happened to me. I had always wanted to do play-by-play earlier in my career, but I had never gotten the opportunity. Not that I was unhappy—I had been given studio hosting assignments that were unprecedented for a woman and my reputation was well established in the business. I was comfortable in my role . . . plus I had just had my first baby. The last thing I needed to do was suddenly tackle a new skill on national television and risk being criticized (not to mention, very stressed out!). Although I had always wanted to do play-by-play, I turned down the assignment twice, before reluctantly agreeing to give it a try. During my hosting stint of the NBA finals that year, I traveled back and forth to WNBA preseason games to practice play-by-play. I was on 11 flights in 14 days to seven different cities! My head was spinning and it was no surprise that I got sick. On the day of the first broadcast, I had to have shots just so I could go on the air without throwing up. I felt terrible and nervous, but I survived my first game. I wasn't very good but gradually, week by week,

I got better. By the end of the season, the TV reviews of my work were much better—*USA Today* called me "most improved."

During that 1997 season, I witnessed a lot of exciting basketball moments, from the first historic game to the first championship, won by the Houston Comets. The challenge of doing play-by-play was really exciting and I loved interviewing the women athletes and seeing the fans' enthusiasm. Over one million fans came to the games; my favorite sight was seeing young boys wearing the jerseys of female players—pretty cool. And to think I almost missed out on all of that. It reinforced the importance of taking chances and not being afraid of challenges or criticism. When we have an opportunity to follow our dreams, we need to go for it!

Thankfully, there are now more opportunities than ever for women in sports (and other areas, like broadcasting). We thank women, like those in this series, who have persevered despite lack of opportunities—women who have refused to see their limitations. Remember, women's sports has been around a long time. Way back in 396 B.C. Kyniska, a Spartan princess, won an Olympic chariot race. Of course, women weren't allowed to compete, so she was not allowed to collect her prize in person. At the 1996 Olympic games in Atlanta, Georgia, over 35,600 women competed, almost a third more than in the previous Summer Games. More than 20 new women's events have been added for the Sydney, Australia, Olympics in 2000. Women's collegiate sports continues to grow,spurred by the 1972 landmark legislation Title IX, which states that "no person in the United States shall, on the basis of sex, be excluded from participation in, be denied the benefits of, or be subjected to discrimination under any educational program or activity receiving federal financial assistance." This has set the stage for many more scholarships and opportunities for women, and now we have professional leagues as well. No longer do the most talented basketball players in the country have to go to Europe or Asia to earn a living.

The women in this series did not have as many opportunities as you have today. But they were persistent through all obstacles, both on the court and off. I can tell you that Cynthia Cooper is the strongest woman I know. What is it that makes Cynthia and the rest of the women included in this series so special? They are not afraid to share their struggles and their stories with us. Their willingness to show us their emotions, open their hearts, bare their souls, and let us into their lives is what, in my mind, separates them from their male counterparts. So accept this gift of their remarkable stories and be inspired. Because you, too, have what it takes to follow your dreams.

1

A DREAM COMES TRUE

Everyone around Anna Kournikova was excited—her coach, her mother, her special friend Sergei Federov—and of course, her many fans.

Anna had just defeated Iva Majoli, the French Open Champion of 1997, in a heated quarterfinal contest at Wimbledon in July 1997. Anna would now compete in the semifinals against her longtime rival, Martina Hingis. By reaching the semifinals, Anna became the second woman from the United States to do so. Chris Evert had been the first.

Anna herself was struck with awe at what she had accomplished. Here she was, a girl from Russia who grew up in very modest circumstances, now competing on the court at Wimbledon. Being here was a dream come true for Anna.

Anna played it cool with reporters. She simply told them, "I like grass, and I have had good results on it," explaining her victory over Majoli. Indeed, sportswriters commented on how quickly Anna adapted to the irregular skips and bounces of the Wimbledon court. Her tennis

Aside from Adidas, Anna also lent her famous name to endorsements for Omega watches. Here she shows off one of the company's new watches in London.

coach, Nick Bollettieri, was happy with what Anna had done. "Anna has no fear," he said. "She keeps coming at you."

Now Anna was looking forward to the upcoming match between her and Martina. It was especially thrilling since it was the second time in 1997 that she and Martina would compete against each other. They had played each other at the French Open, where Hingis won in the third round.

Martina realized how powerful an opponent Anna had become since they played several weeks before at the French Open. Even she admitted that now the stakes were different. "Until now, I always beat her pretty easily," she said. "Tomorrow is going to be a different match. It's another Grand Slam. It's very good for her. She had great results. I never made semifinals by that time, so she beat one of my records now."

Hingis mentioned how she and Anna knew each other from the time they were little, growing up together in the junior tournaments. They always congratulated each other, she recalled, when one of them won or played especially well.

Martina wound up defeating Anna in that semifinal. However, Anna's spirits were not defeated. She realized what an accomplishment it was for a 16-year-old to even play at Wimbledon and, although Anna has played in other Wimbledon tournaments since then, the 1997 match remains one of her fondest—and proudest—memories.

Although her life is filled with glamour and excitement, Anna has to be brave and determined to compete in the high-stakes world of women's tennis. She has to cope with the pres-

Only the second American woman to make it to the semi-finals at Wimbledon, a 16-year-old Anna looked forward to playing her friend and rival, Swiss pro Martina Hingis, on the grass courts. Although Hingis won the match, Anna was proud to have achieved so much at such a young age.

sure, the tension, and the desire to win, and yet not let all this ruffle her when she's playing on the court. Anna has always showed a large amount of bravery and gumption. It was brave of her when she left her native homeland of Russia to come to the United States to study tennis intensively at a special sports academy in Florida. Since then, she has practiced long hours, studied hard, and listened to the criticism of some tough coaches and instructors.

2

THE GIRL FROM MOSCOW

Anna Kournikova was born on Sunday, June 11, 1981, in the city of Moscow. Russia is the largest country in the whole world. Moscow has more than eight million people and is the largest city in Russia. The year Anna was born, 1981, marked another important event for women's tennis. That was the year Tracy Austin won the U. S. Open. She was just 19 years old.

Anna's parents were both talented athletes. Her father Sergei was a Greco-Roman wrestling champion when he was young. He later taught physical education at college. Anna's mother, Alla, was a former 400-meter runner. So both parents passed on their athletic gifts to Anna. Alla was married when she was just 18 years old. When Anna is asked if she also wants to get married young, she always gives a quick "No!"

Today, Anna is a multi-millionaire, not only from winning prize money at tournaments but also because of all her endorsement deals with companies like Lycos, Adidas and Yonex. But her early years growing up in Moscow were

Anna's mother, Alla, has always been a powerful guiding force in Anna's life and career. Here they are together at the Nick Bollettieri Tennis Academy when Anna was only 10.

The daughter of two accomplished athletes, Anna grew up in the Russian capital of Moscow, where she and her parents shared a small apartment downtown. Here is one of Moscow's best-known landmarks, St. Basil's Cathedral on Red Square.

simple and sometimes hard. She and her parents didn't have a lot of money. Anna and her family lived in a small apartment in one of the many drab, large apartment buildings that dot the residential part of Moscow. The large houses that so many people have in the United States are not at all common in Russia. So, while Anna's life wasn't especially rich or glamorous, it was like that of most of the other Russian kids she knew.

Anna received her first tennis racquet as a Christmas gift when she was just five years old.

Her parents had sold their television set to buy it for her. She started playing at a club near her home after school. Soon, she found she enjoyed tennis and was good at it. So she began practicing her game at least twice a week. Right away, tennis became one of Anna's passions.

Although life wasn't easy for Anna and her parents, Anna strongly believes that her years in Russia helped build her character and determination. "In Russia, except for culture, history, books, and museums, you never have anything else. It makes [for] an iron character. Especially if you want to do something with your life. I'm one of those who does want to. Since my childhood, I understood that without a character, you'll never make it."

She says she can't really put her finger on why tennis became so important to her or why she began to focus on it as a career. Nor can her parents explain why they encouraged her to play and practice and to consider competing in it professionally. But, Anna says, "My parents took me to a sports club, because they wanted me to grow healthy."

Like other kids who hope to become star athletes, Anna soon decided on role models in women's tennis. "When I was little," she recalled, "I liked watching Monica Seles and Steffi Graf play. I really liked their style of playing and I labored not to miss a single match when they were playing, [that was] shown on the television. Especially when they played each other."

And so Anna became quite dedicated to her tennis playing. Anna was determined to become a great tennis player. From the beginning, Anna had no doubts about her ability to become successful. She felt she had what it

After moving with her mother to Florida, Anna enrolled in the prestigious Nick Bollettieri Tennis Academy. With Bollettieri as her coach, Anna sharpened her skills and prepared for life on the pro circuit.

took to excel in the world of women's tennis. She always had amazing self-confidence, even before she became a teenager. She credits her parents with teaching her the value of hard work, perseverance, and discipline. "My parents are simply awful," she says with an impish grin. She's just joking, of course. And then she becomes serious about their influence on her.

"There's probably no other girl in the world like me who had so much lessons to learn. Mama, for example, taught me to work a lot. We have a saying here in Russia, 'Who gets up early, God gives him.' It means, 'If you labor very much, then the success will come for sure.' And Daddy, he was always saying that I'm the prettiest girl in the world. Anyway, I am very similar to him."

Anna was seven years old when she entered her very first tennis tournament. She then enrolled in a special sports academy called Spartek. At Spartek, she practiced tennis for several hours a day. The training became much more intense. Just a year later, she won her first tournament. "I watched a lot of tennis on television," Anna told a reporter. "I thought I could go there, too, to the pro tour. But I didn't think it would happen so fast."

An important man in the world of tennis noticed Anna and her amazing ability. The man's name was Gene Scott. He was responsible for organizing a competition called The Kremlin Cup, and it was there that he first saw Anna and experienced her power as an athlete. Scott was publisher of *Tennis Week* magazine. He had set up the tournament as a means to invite the local talent in Russia and to discover which players might be good enough to become professionals.

She was just eight years old, but Anna played so well that Scott was very impressed. He recalls the first time he saw Anna, "She was better than Chrissie (Evert) or Jenny (Capriati) or Tracy (Austin) were." But he adds with a laugh, Anna had a kind of "spoiled" air about her even back then. "People would make a fuss over her," Scott said. "One time she and another girl were hitting against two guys, and she just drilled it at them. She'd hit them and laugh."

It was Scott who introduced Anna to someone who would prove to bring about a dramatic change in her life. Scott told a sports agent named Paul Theofanous from International Management Group (IMG) all about Anna. Theofanous was equally dazzled with Anna.

Before she was ten years old, Anna was signed to a major sports agency for representation and management. They would give her advice on her career and her business prospects. Anna was the youngest athlete, male or female, to be signed by IMG. IMG is one of the biggest sports representation agencies in the world and boasts an incredible list of clients, such as Tiger Woods, Rebecca Romjin-Stamos, and Venus and Serena Williams, to name a few.

That was just the beginning of a whole new life for Anna. In February 1992, when Anna was only ten, she and her mother moved from Russia to live in Florida. With much misgiving and sadness, her father stayed behind to continue his job. Anna and her mother had a tearful farewell session at the Moscow airport with Sergei before they boarded the plane that was to take them to America. Anna still gets choked up when she remembers that scene.

"My daddy was holding me so tight and I kept saying how much I loved him. But he was very loving and encouraging, just like he's always been. He patted my hair and told me that this was the best thing for me, that this was the way for me to become a really important tennis player. Sometimes, he told me, you have to hurt a little bit to reach for something you really want. And he was right. I still miss my father a lot but I get to see him more now because I travel around the world so much for my promotional work and also to play in different tournaments."

Anna and her mother settled in Bradenton, Florida, a picturesque resort town close to Sarasota and St. Petersburg on the state's western shore. It has beautiful white-sand beaches and quaint Spanish-style buildings—

and, more importantly for Anna, it boasts an esteemed tennis school. There she was to study tennis intensively and learn to become a champion.

Even before she became a teenager, Anna was well on her way to becoming one of the biggest female stars in tennis. Many changes and opportunities were ahead of her and she was eager and excited to meet them.

3

MAKING A SPLASH IN THE U.S.A.

Anna was only ten years old when she and her mother moved all the way from Russia to the United States. It was so far to go, and Anna was still a little girl.

Their new home in Bradenton, Florida, was very different from Moscow. Moscow is more like New York or Chicago—a big city with lots of hustle and bustle, crowded streets, and sophisticated people. In contrast, Bradenton had only about 40,000 people and seemed more like a small town. But Bradenton did have one very important claim to fame. It is the site of the Nick Bollettieri Tennis Academy—one of the most respected and well-known tennis academies in the United States, perhaps even in the world. Anna came to study there because her agents at International Management Group (IMG) felt she could learn the most from Bollettieri and his staff.

Nick Bollettieri helps to guide gifted young tennis players on to greatness and victories at the important tennis contests, like Wimbledon and the U.S. Open. Nick Bollettieri is very skilled at helping his students realize

At only 13 years of age, Anna was already a skilled player on the courts, earning high marks on the junior circuit.

Tennis coach Nick Bollettieri knows how to get the best from his stars. Seven number-one players, including Martina Navratilova, have graduated from his school. Here he and Barbara Becker (wife of pro Boris Becker) watch a men's singles match at Wimbledon.

their genius and make the most of their God-given abilities. He turns young prodigies into the winners they are supposed to be. It's no surprise that no fewer than seven number-one players, including Martina Navratilova, have come out of his school.

Although it was over ten years ago that Nick first met Anna Kournikova, he still remembers her arrival and their first meeting quite vividly. "This little girl walks on the court and there's no two ways about it. She knew who she was, and she wanted all the attention," he recalls. Nick realized that she was going to be a star right then—she had radiance and a sense of power about her.

After all, Anna was already making head-lines. Her arrival from Moscow had put her in the public eye. It's not every day that a young Russian girl is brought to the United States, all expenses paid, to study at a top-notch tennis school. Even Anna remembers the press. She says with a little laugh, "When I was like 9, I was in *The New York Times.* When I was 12, every little girl in Russia was trying to wear her hair like mine and playing tennis."

Bollettieri remembers also that although Anna was very talented at tennis, she was also impatient. He felt he had to rein her in, slow her down, and help her learn to be more patient. If he could teach her that, he knew she would become a better tennis player. "Anna," comments Bollettieri, "was very impatient. She had to be the center of attention. We had a little weekend campout, and Anna wanted to know why she had to get her own meal, why she couldn't be served dinner."

Soon after Anna arrived in the United States, she landed the first of what would be many lucrative endorsement deals. She first signed with Adidas (for clothing) and then with the Japanese company Yonex, which manufactures excellent racquets. The deal made Anna a millionaire almost overnight. Anna and her mother couldn't believe their good fortune.

Although Anna wanted to feel at home in her new county, she found everything to be very different from her life in Russia. Sometimes she missed her father, of course, and also her young friends back in Russia. But she never felt that she had abandoned Russia. "I just went to America to train," she once explained to interviewers. "I am Russian but I grew up in America, and this is like my adopted home."

"In Florida," she continues in her sometimes awkward English, "there is everything I need for training: good courts, sun, plentiful vitamin food. Besides, Moscow is a huge city and you need to spend a lot of time for transport. For someone in sport, you need a maximal concentration on your

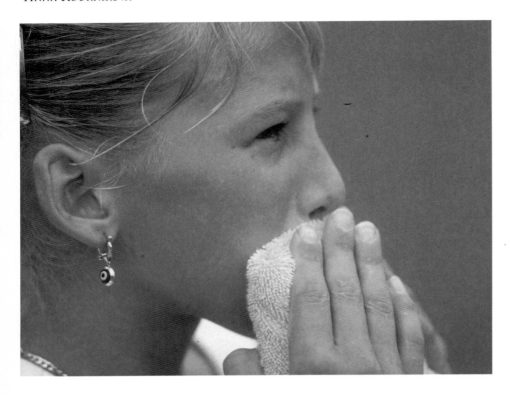

A young Anna takes a break during the 1994 Wimbledon tournament.

training. So Mom and I decided that it was all easier to do in America."

Nowadays, Anna considers herself both Russian and American, actually. She says with a mischievous smile, "I took the best from both countries." In April 1994, Anna made her tennis-playing debut on the Florida junior circuit. There she captured the attention of reporters as she won her first tournament. Just one week later, she was reclassified as the top seed in the division for players 14 years of age and under. (Seed is a term for rank in tennis, as in other sports, like golf.)

One of the first friends Anna made at the Bradenton tennis academy was a boy. She has found it easier to make friends with boys than with girls. The boy who was a friend, but not a boyfriend, was a 13-year-old German named Tommy Haas. Says Haas, "She knew early on she was good-looking and good on the court."

Then, too, Anna and her mother Alla were very close; it was hard for other girls to really get to know her. It was almost as if Alla were enough, and that Anna didn't need the friendship of girlfriends. Alla is Anna's best friend, head coach, mentor, and fun-loving sidekick. To see the two of them with their heads together, both dressed in stunning designer clothes, giggling over a shared secret, you'd think they were sisters.

In fact, Bollettieri has said, "You can't fight Mama, because she and Anna are very close." And another coach has commented, "Alla and Anna are like sister to sister, but sometimes Alla must be the mother and sometimes the father, too."

As a junior player on the tennis circuit, Anna repeatedly beat opponents who were not only older but also considered much more skillful than she was, at least in terms of ranking. In 1995, when she was just 14, Anna represented Russia in a Federation Cup match. She won and became the youngest player ever to win that match. Later that year, she scored another major triumph when she won the prestigious Orange Bowl 18-and-under tournament. A few months later, she won the Italian Junior Open and the European Championship. At the end of 1995, just a little more than three years after her arrival in Florida, Anna was named the ITF Junior World Champion, with a rank of number one.

With all these victories, Anna was anxious and ready to become professional. She would talk about her eagerness to turn pro everytime an interviewer asked her about it. "When do I want to turn pro?" she responded to reporters. "Soon, really soon. The sooner, the better."

Naturally, Anna received a lot of coverage in newspapers and magazines and on television. As she explained, "I've deserved every bit of it. I certainly haven't gotten the attention some players we know have . . . . Venus and Serena Williams (the well-known African-American tennis players) have been given more attention than me, and they haven't even played tournaments. I've put myself on the line. It's not easy to be the number one seed every week with everyone trying to beat you. I've absolutely earned it all."

Finally, Anna turned pro in 1996, much to her relief. It also pleased her ever-increasing number of fans. However, despite her new professional status, she had another restriction imposed on her. A new Women's Tennis Association age restriction was adopted in 1995, limiting her to no more than 16 tournaments a year, until she became 18. So, while Anna was thrilled to be a pro, she was not happy about the restriction.

As she complained, "Venus (Williams) is just coming out, Martina (Hingis) is there. If I could have a little more chance to play, maybe I could be there also." In contrast, Martina Hingis turned pro in 1994, before the new ruling was made. She was only 14 at the time. She was able to play more tournaments and also move up more quickly in the ranks than Anna was able to because she wasn't restricted.

Still, her coach, Nick Bollettieri, was happy with Anna's progress. As he commented a few months after she became pro, Anna is "learning to play with a plan and learning to win. The flagrant errors are starting to disappear. You see more patience now. The performance is getting closer to the ability."

Anna Kournikova was at last in the big leagues in the world of tennis. She was ready to show the world just how much she could do. The waves of "Anna mania," as sports writers started to call the public's infatuation with her, would just keep on growing. Anna was about to become one of the most popular female athletes in the world.

4

COMPETING AS A PRO

Anna Kournikova, professional tennis player! The words made Anna's heart swell with pride. She wanted to do her very best, to rise to the top ranks in women's tennis. One of her first contests as a pro was an ITF Women's Circuit satellite event in the fall of 1996. The contest took place in Midland, Michigan. There she won over other such gifted players as Julie Steven, Jana Nejedly, Rene Simpson, Tami Whitlinger-Jones, and Lindsay Lee.

Right after winning that tournament, Anna boarded a plane and flew to Oklahoma City, Oklahoma. There she won her first-round qualifying match.

Because of these triumphs, Anna was making headlines. She was proclaimed one of the bright new stars in women's tennis. And she was now mentioned along with such other big tennis stars as Martina Hingis, the Williams sisters, and Mirjana Lucic. Coach Bollettieri was excited about her wins and now predicted great things for his student.

Although Anna was defeated in the fourth round of her debut at the U.S. Open by German pro Steffi Graf, she was honored with the title of 1996 Corel WTA Tour Most Impressive Newcomer.

Anna stands with Steffi Graf before their match at the U.S. Open in New York in 1996. Graf won the match 6-2, 6-1.

"I think Anna can hang with any of them," he told *Sports Illustrated.* "Anna is a shot-maker. She has the ability to create situations on the court that very few people can create. And at the net she's brilliant. She hits volleys from all angles. The only person I could compare her to is John McEnroe." (McEnroe was one of the great male tennis players in the 1970s and 1980s. He won many Grand Slam titles.)

Bollettieri wasn't the only one who foresaw a dazzling future for Anna. "Anna can become a superstar of unbelievable magnitude," said

Charlie Pasarell, who had been the top-ranked player in 1967, and today serves as a coach and consultant and runs the Indian Wells tournament. "You can tell she's special just by looking at her. She walks like a champion."

Anna's next big splash as a pro came at the U.S. Open in September 1996. The U.S. Open is one of the four big contests in tennis known as Grand Slams. In addition to the U.S. Open, the other Grand Slams are the Australian Open, the French Open, and Wimbledon—perhaps the most important and prestigious of them all.

At the 1996 U.S. Open, Anna advanced to the fourth round before she was defeated by the eventual champion that year, Steffi Graf. It was a very good performance for her first time at the Open. As a result of all these victories, Anna was named the 1996 Corel WTA Tour Most Impressive Newcomer. But if people were paying more attention to the Russian tennis star, it wasn't just because of her skillful playing. Unfortunately, because of her beauty and all the attention she was getting, some of her fellow female tennis players were a little envious of Anna. They were also jealous of the million-dollar endorsement deals she was getting. IMG had also negotiated a deal for her with Berlei sports bras, from England.

But some of the old-timers in women's tennis were heartened by Anna's success. They felt that women tennis players were at last reaching the same levels as men, commanding headlines and getting fabulous endorsement contracts.

Billie Jean King was one of the best tennis players in the world. She was a huge star in the 1960s and 1970s, won a lot of tournaments and even bested a top male star, Bobby Riggs, in a highly publicized match. But King had almost no endorsement deals. Despite her fame and her skill, she just couldn't get any really significant endorsements. Big companies simply weren't using women for that back then.

Today, Billie Jean is happy about the importance of women's tennis and pleased that players like Anna are getting huge deals. "We have a chance to do what no other women's sport has done—to gain equity with comparable men's sports," observed King. "That's done at the box office. It doesn't bother me at all if some of the guys come out to watch women's tennis because they want to see a beautiful woman. Who can hold that against Anna? Still, it is unfortunate when others with a high skill factor don't win the endorsements. Sure, the good-looking guy gets more endorsements, but the difference in men's sports is that the ugly ones get their share too."

As good as Anna looked on the court, she also played exceptionally well. Anna is an incredibly powerful and gifted player. She has terrific speed and an excellent running forehand where she runs to hit the ball with tremendous force. It requires a lot of skill, a lot of concentration and a perfect or near perfect stroke. The running forehand shot is one of Anna's biggest assets as a tennis player.

Other female pros who have been in the game for some time recognize that Anna has many strengths. As Monica Seles says, "Anna has things that the rest of us don't have, so yes, some of the players are envious of her. But others who know her like her. They all know she works hard. Remember, she comes from a hard place . . . so perhaps Anna should get more credit than some want to give her."

When Anna played at the world famous Wimbledon tournament in 1997, the British newspapers had a field day speculating about her romances and her good looks. She was clearly the most publicized player there. Although Anna was pretty low-key about how she felt about Wimbledon to reporters at the time, she was thrilled to be playing at one of the most important contests in tennis. Wimbledon, located in a southwestern London suburb, has held tennis tournaments since 1886, sponsored by the All-England Tennis and Croquet Club. As Anna confessed to a group of reporters several months after Wimbledon, "Going through the series of Wimbledon was a time that still reigns supreme in the memories of my tennis career today."

She continued, "When I went out on the court and started my first match on the Wimbledon schedule, for a long time I couldn't believe it's true, what is happening. It was a moment I dreamed of my whole life. I was following how all the great matches were played on that court."

Anna progressed to the semifinals at Wimbledon, an impressive achievement for her first time there. Martina Hingis finally defeated her. As a result of her performance at Wimbledon, Anna rose to a number 25 ranking in women's tennis. Her fellow tennis players also seemed very impressed with Anna's playing on the prestigious English court. Said American television sports commentator Mary Carillo, "People acted like it was a fluke, but it really wasn't. She has a beautiful serve, explosive racquet work, and she's the quickest player on the tour. People focus on her hair and her attitude. What's been overlooked is that she's one heck of a tennis player."

However, Martina Hingis was not so impressed. She beat Anna 6-3 and 6-2. Later, when asked about her opponent, she commented, "I don't think it's such a big rivalry. Everybody else is making a big rivalry of it. Until now I've always been better and always beat her at the great tournaments, as I did this time again."

Hingis then continued, "She's very pretty, but I'm sure she would like to change places with me if she could and have four grand Slam titles." Because of remarks like this, and because both Martina and Anna are quite attractive, the press has made much of a supposed heated and strong competition between them. Each time they play each other, it's as though two opposing countries are going to war. And then, neither Martina nor Anna has been particularly gracious about each other. They have each said that they don't think much of the other as a tennis player. In other words, each has the attitude of "She is good, but not nearly as good as I am."

There was another factor in Anna's receiving so much press attention at Wimbledon. After all, one of the fans cheering her on and attending every match was her current boyfriend, Sergei Federov. Sergei is also Russian, and also an important athlete in his own right. He is star center on the Detroit Red Wings hockey team, and is 12 years older than Anna. They were seen together at the All England Club and around the fancy places in London. Naturally, the press made much of their outings, saying that this was apparently Anna's first serious boyfriend.

But Anna protests using the word "boyfriend" in regard to Sergei. As she says with impatience and a toss of that golden head of hair, "In Russia there is no word for boyfriend. You're either married or you're friends. Maybe people want to see Sergei as my boyfriend, but he's just a good friend of mine— a very good friend. Our families are close. We come from the same background, and we have a lot in common."

Anna's mother Alla also pooh-poohed the talk of romance between Sergei and her daughter. "They're friends. It's normal . . . . Federov and Anna have known each other for years, ever since they met on a Moscow tennis court." Just as coy and elusive as her daughter, Alla was never more specific about the date and circumstances of that meeting.

But during the Wimbledon matches, Federov did act very attentively to Anna and seemed very much like a boyfriend, despite Anna's claims to the contrary. The athlete, who recently signed a $38 million contract, was happy to carry her tennis gear around and seemed to cater to her every whim. And Anna was sporting a rather large, fancy diamond ring. Was it from Sergei Federov? In typical Anna fashion, she just laughed when asked the question. She wasn't about to say anything to reporters about that ring. After all, it was her private business.

Both Sergei and Anna have always downplayed the seriousness of their relationship. According to Anna, "Sergei and I have a very nice relationship, but what will become of it only time will show."

As for Sergei, he says, "She's my good friend and why not? We come from exactly the same background. We are professional athletes. Her career is rising; mine is in the middle. We're doing very well."

5

Part of "The Beautiful Brat Pack"

In September 1998, right before the United States Open began in New York City, *Time* magazine ran a story about the huge popularity of women's tennis. According to the article, more attention than ever was being paid to female tennis players and the tournaments they played. In addition, both the printed press and television regularly featured stories on the Tennis Gang of Four, as the magazine called them—Venus Williams, her sister Serena, Martina Hingis, and of course, Anna Kournikova. Much of the increased interest in women's tennis, according to *Time*, had to do with the glamour and playing power of these tennis whiz kids.

Another writer dubbed the Williams sisters, Martina, and Anna as "the Beautiful Brat Pack." And as proof of their widespread appeal, these athletic young women were being featured in such non-sports magazines as *People*, *Vogue*, and *Forbes*. Billie Jean King said that it was "the greatest time in the history of women's tennis."

Anna has always downplayed her relationship with NHL pro and fellow-Russian Sergei Federov, stating that in Russia there is no word for "boyfriend."

At the center of all this attention and fanfare was Anna Kournikova, the golden-haired star from Russia. Indeed, as the U.S. Open began in September, *Sports Illustrated* said, "No player was more gawked at or gossiped about than 17-year-old Anna Kournikova."

But, despite all the attention, Anna emphasized that she was a tennis player, first and foremost. "I'm here because of tennis," she commented to reporters at the U.S. Open. "I'm not a party girl." Anna was the first Russian woman to be seeded at the Open since 1976. Although she didn't capture a singles title at the U.S. Open that year, Anna performed very well. She defeated three opponents and advanced to the fourth round, where Steffi Graf bested her.

Doing well at the U.S. Open that September was just part of a series of victories and triumphs that Anna scored in 1998. In fact, 1998 was a banner year for Anna, a year in which she racked up an impressive array of performances that catapulted her to a top ranking in women's tennis. While it's true that she did not win a singles titles of any kind in 1998, she made it to the semifinals or finals in the top contests. More importantly, she defeated some of the biggest stars in women's tennis that year.

One of her biggest triumphs was over her archrival Martina Hingis. She beat Martina in the quarterfinals at the German Open in August 1998. The defeat marked Martina's first professional loss to a younger player. That victory enabled Anna to move up to an impressively high ranking of 13 in women's tennis, the highest she'd achieved so far.

Travel is a big part of being a tennis pro. Here Anna signs autographs for fans at the Toyota Princess Cup women's tournament in Tokyo, Japan.

During the other contests between her and Hingis that year, although Anna didn't win, she played hard games against Martina and gave the Czech star a run for her money. In the third round of the Australian Open, in January 1998, she stretched Martina to three sets, before losing 6-4, 4-6, and 6-4.

Sports writers and commentators were saying that Anna was finally playing the kind of tennis she had shown only flashes of before— she was playing the best she had since she turned pro in 1995. Anna, they wrote, was maturing into the type of player who could make it into the very top levels, the top five or even number one. At the Lipton contest in Key Biscayne, Florida in December 1998, Anna defeated four top ten players—in just four days. The Lipton is considered a sort of unofficial fifth Grand Slam and is always held at the end of the year. The first player Anna vanquished was none other than her idol as a young girl, Monica Seles. She beat Monica 7-5, 6-4. Seles was gracious about the defeat and quite impressed with Anna's playing. As she commented to reporters, "She kept it together the whole match . . . I think she can be a top five player—and maybe number one."

Then Anna proceeded to trounce Conchita Martinez and Lindsay Davenport, who was then ranked number two in women's tennis. Lindsay was also awed by Anna's game. "She hits the ball so hard," she said after the match. "She's aggressive; she comes to the net a lot more than most girls do."

Then, in the semifinals, Anna beat Arantxa Sanchez-Vicario, an outstanding player from Spain who ranked number eight. An ecstatic Anna was very proud of how well she was playing. She crowed to reporters, "Wow! This is great! I'm playing! I didn't try to go for winners right away! I kept the ball in play three, four, five times and I went for it when I had a good shot. I proved to everyone that I can play tennis, a lot of matches in a row."

Anna's new coach, Pavel Slozil, who counts Steffi Graf among his former pupils, was also pleased with Anna's performance. He told reporters that Anna was definitely improving. But more importantly for her game in the long run, Slozil said, "She's more focused, more confident. Beating four great tennis players in one week is confirmation that she's not just a one-day player."

Some tennis fans will go to any length to support their favorite stars. At the 1998 Australian Open, two men in the stands dress as Anna and cheer her on in her match against Martina Hingis.

Pavel also addressed the criticism other females have of Anna. He doesn't think of her as arrogant or spoiled. "I think she is a good kid," he said. "But for sure there are many people happy if she loses. If someone is better-looking or has more money, well, jealousy is jealousy."

As 1998 drew to a close, Anna found herself qualifying for the season-ending Chase Championships in both singles and doubles. At that time, she had earned a ranking as number 16 as a singles player and in the top eight doubles category, paired with Larisa Neiland. No matter whether she won or lost, there were always the wild displays of "Annamania" wherever she played. At the Australian Open, there was a big battle off the court among Anna's fans for a piece of her gear. In the midst of a warm-up, a group of spectators scrambled to grab one of the towels Anna had just wiped her face with. Then there was the group of male fans who proudly held a banner each time Anna came on the court. The banner said, in big letters, "Anna, will you marry me?"

If Anna was disturbed by these antics, she never let on. In fact, she always maintained her characteristic poise and sense of humor. Commenting on the banner, she said, "The only questions I had was 'Which one? Should I marry all of them?'"

1998 marked another big landmark for Anna. She decided to leave the sports talent agency IMG, the management group that had signed her up when she was just a little girl in Russia and had brought her and her mother to the United States. Anna made a new deal with a management group called Advantage International Sports Agency. As with any major news about Anna, there was quite a bit of controversy over it. IMG, in fact, was said to be very angry about Anna's leaving. What made matters worse was that Anna's good friend Sergei Federov was also moving to Advantage. His decision to leave IMG came just a short while after IMG had negotiated a new contract for him that paid the Russian hockey star center $38 million for playing in 43 games for the Detroit Red Wings.

Anna was quick to defend her move to the press. She said, "It's just that they [IMG] have too many players and too many responsibilities. How can a person manage you when he's not with you at a Grand Slam or not there when you beat the number one player or for your first top ten win? When I beat Steffi Graf (in 1998), my agent wasn't there." (For his part, her agent explained his absence by saying that Monica Seles' father had just died).

In making the announcement of Anna's new long-term contract with Advantage, president Phil de Piccioto talked about finally "stressing her tennis skills in all her promotion work because that is what makes Anna attractive." In other words, what he was really saying was that Advantage wasn't going to focus on Anna's physical beauty but instead play up her powerful athletic ability and her tennis skills. Advantage would promote the conservative side of Anna, the girl who says she only kisses on dates and believes very strongly in God. Anna once confided, "I like to go to church. It's so nice and peaceful inside. You come out and you feel clean. Everything dirty is gone."

Part of Advantage's game plan was to squash the impression that Anna was self-absorbed and not interested in anything beyond herself and tennis. Advantage was going to make sure that the serious and thoughtful side of Anna came out. After all, the Russian teen is very intelligent—her father is a college professor. She thinks carefully about current events. She has said, "I'm concerned . . . about war. There is enough place for everyone in the world. Why can't they just talk—not with tanks and guns?

Why did they send those Russian kids to die in Afghanistan? They didn't even live to die yet. How many mothers are crying out there? There's not even a cemetery to know where their bodies are."

Still, there were other factors that spurred Anna to leave IMG for Advantage. Some of these were not so widely publicized at the time. It was said that Anna felt another IMG client, Martina Hingis, her longtime rival, was getting more attention—and more lucrative endorsement deals. Martina had recently landed very profitable deals with Clairol and Ocean Spray. But what could have been more upsetting to Anna was the fact that Martina landed the cover of *Gentlemen's Quarterly*. She became the first female athlete to make the cover of that well-respected men's magazine. It was the kind of publicity that Anna would have enjoyed. (Just two years later, however, Anna also made the cover of *GQ*).

Since joining Advantage, Anna has landed some impressive endorsement deals herself. They negotiated for her to represent Charles Schwab, an investment counseling firm, and Pegaso, a cell-phone communications company based in Mexico. There's a definite plan behind Anna's deals with companies based outside the United States. As de Piccioto puts it, "We want to make Anna global. We want to make her a player known the world over." And meanwhile, Anna keeps working on her tennis, knowing full well that as a spokesperson for all these companies, it's crucial that she be the best player she can.

She says, "I can do it all—the volley, the lob, the drop shot, slices, topspin, moving, anything . . . I don't feel fear out there. I think I can hit anything I want."

Some people may find that kind of comment arrogant or conceited. But other gifted athletes understand what Anna is saying and where she is coming from. Anna is showing her confidence and her fearlessness in her game—and that's an important part of being a star and a winner in sports.

6

A GRAND SLAM TITLE AT LAST!

In January 1999, at the Australian Open, Anna captured one of the sweetest victories in her whole career. Paired with former archrival Martina Hingis, the unlikely duo defeated the team of Lindsay Davenport and Natasha Zvereva in the doubles final and won the Grand Slam title. It was the first—and so far the only—time Anna won a Grand Slam. She was thrilled. She also performed well as a single, advancing to the fourth round before being defeated by Mary Pierce.

The pairing of Anna and Martina as a doubles team showed a newfound maturity on Anna's part. It showed that she was willing to overlook the battles between them as singles players in the past and a desire to forget the cutting remarks they had traded in the press. Most importantly, it proved that Anna had grown not only as a tennis player, but also as a person.

The fact is, although they have been pitted against each other on the court, Anna Kournikova and Martina Hingis have a lot in common. Both are European-born and live in America. Both are certainly superstars in their game. Both

The doubles victory in Australia earned Anna and partner Martina Hingis a Grand Slam trophy and a furry friend—a little toy kangaroo.

have been known to display temper tantrums on the court, stomping their feet and throwing racquets around when they're disappointed in their performances. And both are very attractive. In fact, Martina has said that she once toyed with the idea of becoming a model until tennis got in her blood and she could no longer think of any other career.

It seemed, too, that Martina was happy to be paired with a tennis star like Anna who had so much glamour. Giggling to reporters, Martina referred to herself and Anna as "the tennis Spice Girls." She showed that she could provide quips for the press when the situation called for it. In fact, Anna and Martina put on a darling act for the fans. They high-fived each other after points gained during the match. Once the game was won, they took souvenirs from their tennis gear and threw them into the crowd. Finally, for almost half an hour after the game was over, they signed autograph after autograph.

Reporting on the match, *Tennis* magazine said that Hingis was "a good tennis influence on Kournikova, settling Kournikova's fragile nerves, boosting her confidence in her oft-errant serve and helping her capture her first major title." But Kournikova was also helpful to Martina. After Martina made a blunt and not-too-complimentary remark about another female tennis player to the press, which greatly embarrassed her later, it was Anna who comforted her and gave her some good advice on dealing with reporters. She told Martina, obviously drawing on her own considerable experience over the years, "There is an old Russian saying that you cannot spit in the well from which you drink. You have to be more diplo-

Doubles tennis demands a special level of skill and teamwork. Here, Anna and doubles partner Martina Hingis share a bow for the crowd after their victory in the 1999 Australian Open doubles final.

matic with the press. You cannot say these things."

After Anna gave Martina those words of advice, the Czech star was able to talk with the press and act more regretful, instead of stubborn and defiant, as she would have before. It's apparent that both Martina and Anna, thrown into the public eye before they fully matured and while they were still very young, have had to learn how to conduct themselves like adults. Anna has come a long way from the days when she used to brag to reporters about her ability and say things that made her seem foolish and conceited in print. Anna, it seems, has been growing up with a good head on her shoulders, in spite of all the pressure and tension she faces every week as a world-famous contender in women's tennis.

Anna, of course, was pleased with her Australian Open doubles win. However, she is still hoping for a Grand Slam title as a singles player. The year 1999 was an up-and-down year for her in terms of tournaments. Despite a troublesome serve, she won the opening round of the Australian Open tournament for singles. She then beat favorite Jennifer Capriati at the Bausch and Lomb tournament in April. But then at the Family Circle Cup, Martina Hingis handily dispatched her in April at the posh resort of Hilton Head, South Carolina. Three months later, despite a crowd wildly cheering her on and yelling, "Anna, Anna," she suffered an unexpected defeat from Amanda Coetzer during the semifinals of the A & P Tennis Classic in July, even though it seemed that the statuesque Russian would easily overwhelm Coetzer, a tiny 5 feet 2 inches tall. A sprained foot kept Anna out of the tour for several weeks in fall 1999, but she returned in October to defeat Cara Black of Zimbabwe in the first round of the Generali Ladies Tournament in Linz, Austria. However, at the season-ending Chase Championships at Madison Square Garden in New York City, Anna was beaten in a close match by Mary Pierce.

Although the press constantly mentions the fact that Anna has yet to win a singles title, she herself is confident that her day will come. She knows that her game is getting better all the time. Anna acquired a new coach in 1999, a Dutchman named Eric Van Harpen. Van Harpen has helped her perfect her game and is grooming her to be at the top of her form. He admits that he's strict with Anna, even "hard" on her. But this is to help her improve, not to shake her confidence. He tells her, "Sure you are a beautiful girl, but there are enough of them in the world. But, Anna, there has never been a beautiful girl who can win at tennis."

Some observers think that Anna's beauty is a deterrent to her tennis-playing ability. No less a tennis superstar than Tracy Austin said, when asked about the one thing that could work against Anna's reaching the top in tennis, "Because she is so comfortable in the limelight, she could have trouble staying focused. Playing on the circuit a number of years will help. When you have a terrific personality, you have to remember to concentrate on your game. If Kournikova can do both, that's the key."

That is what Van Harpen is teaching Anna to do, and it seems to be working. As she told a writer from *Gentlemen's Quarterly*, when she is on the tennis court, nothing else matters. She says she is "just thinking about the ball that's coming at me, just in my own world." Then she adds, "I have to have a wall around me, which is pretty hard, but I'm used to it."

But Anna also believes that her many profitable endorsement deals and her looks make her draw more fire from the press and criticism from others. She says, "There are a lot of pretty girls, cute girls, whatever, out there. If I'd be 500, nobody would know. It's that I have a good personality and am a good tennis player. That's what creates this situation." And Anna adds, "What should I do, make myself ugly? It's that I'm pretty that I have this problem. I am who I am."

Anna isn't the only tennis player to suffer from off-the-court business and commitments. Martina Hingis, thought to be the sure winner in the Grand Slams in 1998, didn't win a single tournament during a six-month stretch. Her decline in power playing was probably because of the demands of her endorsement deals. When asked about her losses, she confessed quietly, "I learned I should not shoot so many commercials the week before a Grand Slam."

It's not easy being a top-ranked, highly-paid female athlete. One day Anna is in Chile, South America, and the next day she's jetting off to Canada. That's why, when a reporter asked where she lives full-time, Anna said, "I travel fulltime." Anna's life is very different from other teenagers'. She doesn't know what it's like to goof off or hang out with friends, or go bopping around a mall. Her former coach at Bradenton, Nick Bollettieri said, "Sometimes Anna must be lost. She never had a childhood. She must wonder what it's like to live a normal life."

But Anna bristles at this talk and denies that she's missing out on anything. Despite all the pressure and the constant traveling and the scrutiny of the public she insists that she's quite happy. "What is normal?" she asks. "That kind of life everybody talks about as 'normal' wouldn't be normal for me. From age five, when I first played tennis, that's all I wanted. From the first I was so happy on the tennis court. I can't think of anything better."

And there are times when Anna, like other teenagers, gets to do "real people" things. She loves going out to eat at restaurants. For those brief moments, she could be any other girl, going out to eat, savoring her favorite dish. Then, she's no longer Anna the celebrity, but Anna the high-spirited teenager with that golden hair trailing down her back.

Some of Anna's favorite foods are sushi, French fries, and chocolate. She loves chocolate in any form, whether it's cake, candy or a milkshake. In fact, Eric Van Harpen has been known to use chocolate to motivate Anna. He tells her if she hits a certain number of balls or pitches her serve a certain way so many times, she'll be rewarded with a chocolate treat. Van Harpen says, for Anna, the promise of a chocolate treat is a great motivator.

There are other tricks Van Harpen uses to improve Anna's game. Sometimes he raises the net a few inches during practice. Then he covers the net with blankets so Anna can't see through. This way, he says, "She can't see it until it's over the net. It forces her to react faster with both her eyes and her feet."

Van Harpen also preaches the importance of avoiding negativity and replacing bad attitudes with positive thinking. She is told not to read articles that talk about how she's never won a singles title. "Don't listen to what others think of you or your game," Van Harpen tells her.

And so Anna has learned how to tune all the critical and negative stuff out. She possesses a great deal of emotional and inner strength. Van Harpen wants Anna to build on this strength to be the best tennis player she can be. It's more important to Anna than anything else. She wants to be the champion she knows she was born to be.

THE BEST IS YET TO COME

It was the beginning of the year 2000, and Anna Kournikova found herself accepting another trophy. Only this award wasn't for winning a tournament and didn't really involve her tennis playing. Anna received the Lycos.com award for being the most searched-for female athlete in the entire world. It's estimated that some 18,000 web pages are devoted to Anna. Her official site is www.kournikova.com. But, at any given moment, someone somewhere is downloading a website to find out more about the pretty Russian tennis ace.

Anna was thrilled to accept the award. "I think it's pretty amazing," she commented later. "It's really exciting. And when I got the trophy, it was really pretty." Then mindful of the loyalty of her many fans, she added, "I would like to thank my fans, who look me up on the Internet. It's what made it possible for me to be number one there."

Later that year, in August, Anna scored another important victory on the courts. She defeated top-ranked Lindsay Davenport at the Acura Classic in Carlsbad, California. It was an especially meaningful triumph for

Soon after arriving from Russia, young Anna was approached by Adidas sportswear to become a spokesperson for their products. This endorsement deal, along many others she would sign, meant a big payday for Anna, seen here autographing her 2001 Roland Garros outfit in Paris.

Always appreciative of her fans and coach, Anna blows a kiss after a victory in the first round of the 2000 Australian Open.

Anna, since Lindsay had defeated her three different times during 1999. Lindsay was then ranked second in women's tennis, so the win increased her standing in women's tennis. Anna's rank rose to number nine.

In October 2000 a group of some of the world's best tennis players, including the super-talented Williams sisters, went to compete in the 2000 Olympics in Sydney, Australia. Anna, however, did not attend the games. Instead she played in the Luxembourg Open, where she was ranked as the top seed. There she beat Nadeja Petrova and then defeated defending champion Kim Clijsters in the quarterfinals. In a surprising upset, however, seventh-seeded Magdalena Maleeva defeated Anna, in her third match. She didn't seem to be very upset over the loss and reacted with dignity and composure. She said, "Everybody is here to win, and she (Magdalena) was playing better than me today. I tried to give my best."

These days, Anna seems to take defeats with a lot more coolness—no more temper tantrums for her. Anna seems to take the position that when she loses, it doesn't mean that she's not as good a player as the woman who defeats her. It simply means in Anna's mind that the other woman was playing better tennis that day. Perhaps that is part of the positive attitude philosophy that her coach, Eric Van Harpen, tries to instill in her. For example, after a loss to Venus Williams in Key Biscayne, Florida, she said, "I think I just got a little bit tired physically. But it's good. It shows me that she didn't beat me; I lost. That means I'm better, a little bit better, than her."

It's an attitude that might seem cocky, but it probably gives Anna hope and prevents her from being depressed and sad over a loss. It's also undoubtedly a motivator for her to play better the next time. As the first year of the new millennium came to a close, Anna experienced some difficulties. The first happened when her slated doubles partner Martina Hingis dumped her. Although the official reason given was that Martina wanted to cut back on her doubles commitments, it was said that what really happened was a fight between the two during an exhibition match in Chile in late November. Martina did play doubles with Monica Seles at the Australian Open a few weeks later.

Then, just before Christmas, there was quite a commotion on a commercial set in Key Biscayne, Florida. Anna was supposed to be photographed for an advertisement for Lycos Fantasy Sport, a line of sportswear for women. However, she arrived almost six hours late. Anna was quite upset even after her arrival, and she argued with the photographer about an outfit she was supposed to wear for the photo shoot. Anna thought it was too "skimpy." So she refused to pose in that particular costume. Even though there was a lot of pressure and tension on the set, Anna bravely stuck to her principles.

But the year 2000 brought one major source of happiness to Anna. In December, she bought a new home for her mother in Miami Beach, Florida. The house, which cost $5.2 million, is an eye-catching showplace with seven bedrooms, seven baths, a five-room guesthouse, and yacht moorings. It's a big change from the two-room apartment where Anna spent her childhood in Moscow.

Anna recently made another handsome endorsement deal with Omega, a company that makes beautiful, expensive watches. She will be featured in print advertisements and outdoor boards to introduce a new line of gold watches with pastel-colored bands. The new line is called "Constellation Carre." Other celebrities who have helped to promote Omega watches in the past are supermodel Cindy Crawford and actor Pierce Brosnan.

According to Raquel L. Schuttler, the director of marketing for Omega, Anna was chosen for her "fashionable image and athletic renown." Anna enjoys representing such a prestigious line of product. And, like any other person, she loves wearing the beautiful watches.

Meanwhile, her tennis playing continues to improve. While she has yet to win a singles title, she has made it into the quarterfinals or semifinals at tournaments in 2001. At the Australian Open, Anna made the quarterfinals before being beaten by Lindsay Davenport. Lindsay again beat Anna at the Pan Pacific

Open, but Anna did make it into the fourth round for that contest. In February 2001 she made it to the quarterfinals at the Open Gaz de Paris, and then was defeated by local favorite Amelie Mauresmo. It was an upset for Anna, since she seemed to be in control and primed for victory in their opening set.

As another example of her rising stature, Anna was seeded number one in singles for the first time ever in a WTA-sponsored event in Acapulco, Mexico. However, she suffered a stress fracture in her foot and had to withdraw from playing. She had to miss tournaments in Mexico and Indian Wells in California. But, despite being sidelined with the foot injury, Anna received very good news in the beginning of April. The World Team Tennis draft was held on April 3, 2001, and Anna received a ranking of number eight. It was another indicator of Anna's high standing in tennis.

Another big achievement for Anna was that she was selected to play in the DuPont World Team Tennis Professional League in summer 2001, along with other top stars like Serena Williams, Jan-Michael Gambill, and Monica Seles. In March 2001 *Forbes* magazine featured an article on the "Power Celebrities." The article ranked Anna at number 73, with a yearly income estimated to be about $10 million from tournaments but mostly from endorsements.

For now, playing tennis is what seems to be uppermost on Anna's mind, though she confesses to considering a career in modeling or some sort of television work in the future. She gives you that dazzling smile, tosses her blond braid over her shoulder and walks with confidence and pride into the sunlight. Anna Kournikova walks and acts like a champion, so it would be no surprise if she becomes number one.

STATISTICS

Year	Wins	Losses	
1995	6	3	
1996	22	8	
1997	17	10	
1998	40	20	
1999	35	19	
2000	47	29	

Grand Slam titles:	1 doubles
Grand Slam titles:	0 singles
ITF Women's Circuit singles titles:	2
WTA Tour singles titles:	0
WTA Tour doubles titles:	12
2000 Prize Money:	$984,930
Career Prize Money:	$2,692,929

CHRONOLOGY

1981	Anna Kournikova is born in Moscow, Russia, on June 7 to Alla and Sergei Kournikova
1986	Anna receives a tennis racquet for Christmas and starts playing at a local youth center
1988	Anna enters her first tennis tournament and enrolls in a special sports academy called Spartek
1990	Anna signs a contract with IMG
1992	Anna and her mother move to Bradenton, Florida; begins studies at the Nick Bollettieri Tennis Academy
1995	Anna wins Orange Bowl 18 and under contest and the European Championships for 18-and-under; she becomes a semifinalist at Wimbledon juniors; she becomes a quarterfinalist at the French Open for juniors
1996	Anna wins the Federation Cup competition, representing Russia; she becomes the youngest player ever to compete and win in the Fed Cup; turns pro; she wins her first professional title at ITF Women's Circuit satellite event; she plays in her first Grand Slam tournament and reaches the fourth round
1997	Anna debuts at Wimbledon as a professional and becomes the second woman from the U.S. the Open era to reach the Wimbledon semifinals; her ranking moves up to no. 25, the highest so far; she defeats three top ten players, including Arantxa Sanchez-Vicario, Iva Majoli, and Anke Huber
1998	Anna wins first WTA Tour professional title at the Princess Cup in Tokyo, by winning the doubles crown with Monica Seles; she defeats Steffi Graf at Eastbourne and has ranking move up to top ten; she defeats No. 1 ranked Martina Hingis in quarterfinals at German Open; she defeats four top ten players in four days at Lipton; named one of *People Weekly*'s 50 Most Beautiful People along with Leonardo di Caprio; acquires Pavel Slovik as new coach
1999	Anna wins first Grand Slam title at Australian Open, playing doubles with Martina Hingis; reaches fourth round in singles at Wimbledon; ends 1999 as the world's no.1-ranked doubles player; acquires new coach, Eric Van Harpen
2000	Anna reaches doubles semifinals at Wimbledon; tears a ligament in her left ankle at German Open, keeping her off the tour for several weeks; stretches no. 2 Martina Hingis to three sets in quarterfinals at Hamburg, Germany; buys new house in Miami Beach for $5.2 million
2001	Anna named most searched for female athlete on the world wide web and receives Lycos.com award; WTA names her no. 8 in ranking (her highest rank to date); *Forbes* magazine names her among the top 100 most powerful and money-making celebrities

INDEX

FURTHER READING

Aronson, Virginia. *Venus Williams*. Philadelphia: Chelsea House Publishers, 1999.

Ashe, Arthur. *Getting Started In Tennis*. New York: Atheneum, 1977.

Gilbert, Nancy. *Wimbledon*. Mankato, Minnesota: Creative Education, Inc., 1990.

Goldstein, Margaret J. *Jennifer Capriati: Tennis Sensation*. Minneapolis: Lerner Publications Company, 1993.

Jensen, Julie. *Beginning Tennis*. Minneapolis: Lerner Publications Company, 1995.

Knapp, Ron. *Sports Great Steffi Graf*. Springfield, New Jersey: Enslow Publisher, 1995.

Leder, Jane Mersky. *Martina Navratilova*. Mankato, Minnesota: Crestwood House, 1985.

Miller, Marc. *Fundamental Tennis*. Minneapolis: Lerner Publications Company, 1995.

Schwabacher, Martin. *Superstars of Women's Tennis*. Philadelphia: Chelsea House Publishers, 1997.

ABOUT THE AUTHOR

CONNIE BERMAN is a writer and editor who has worked on more than 20 books about celebrities in movies, television, music, sports and politics. Her subjects include Mel Gibson, Tom Cruise, Linda Ronstadt, Michael J. Fox, John F. Kennedy Jr. and Dolly Parton. She also writes cookbooks, including one on yogurt and one on bagels. Connie was the coproducer of *The Yuppie Handbook: A Guide for Young Urban Professionals* (Simon & Schuster). She lives outside Philadelphia and is currently working on a novel.

HANNAH STORM, NBC Sports play-by-play announcer, reporter, and studio host, made her debut in 1992 at Wimbledon during the All England Tennis Championships. Shortly thereafter, she was paired with Jim Lampley to cohost the *Olympic Show* for the 1992 Olympic Games in Barcelona. Later that year, Storm was named cohost of *Notre Dame Saturday*, NBC's college football pregame show. Adding to her repertoire, Storm became a reporter for the 1994 Major League All-Star Game and the pregame host for the 1995, 1997, and 1999 World Series. Storm's success as host of *NBA Showtime* during the 1997–98 season won her the role as studio host for the inaugural season of the Women's National Basketball Association in 1998.

In 1996, Storm was selected as NBC's host for the Summer Olympics in Atlanta, and she has been named as host for both the 2000 Summer Olympics in Sydney and the 2002 Winter Olympics in Salt Lake City. Storm received a Gracie Allen Award for Outstanding Personal Achievement, which was presented by the American Women in Radio and Television Foundation (AWRTF), for her coverage of the 1999 NBA Finals and 1999 World Series. She has been married to NBC Sports broadcaster Dan Hicks since 1994. They have two daughters.